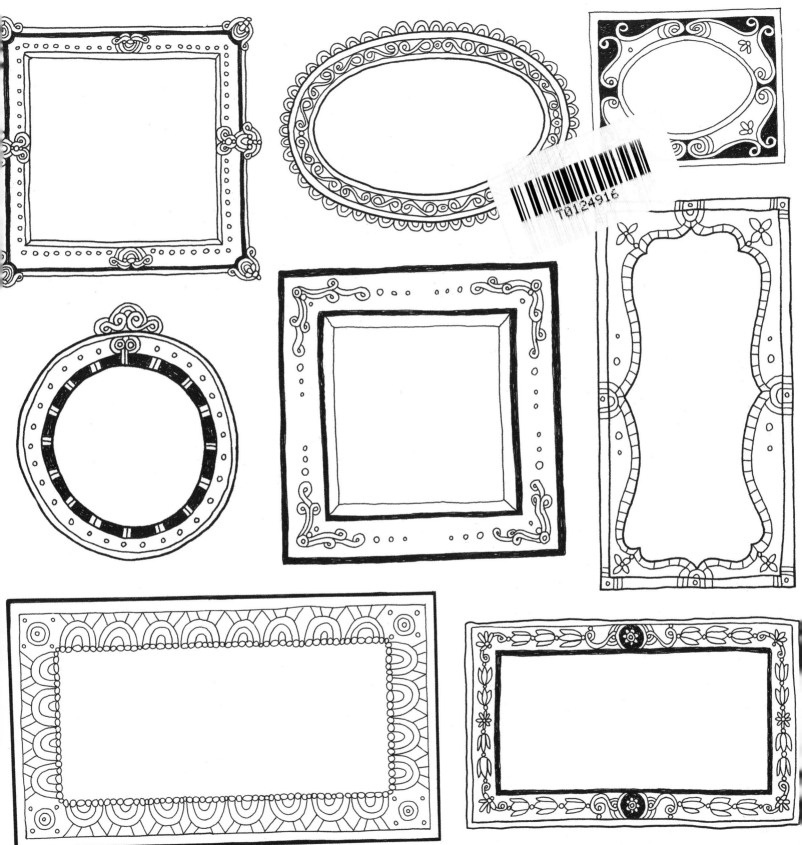

FOR JEN
WITH SPECIAL THANKS TO LINDSEY, LINDA
MEG, SARAH AND COLIN

AN ART ADVENTURE

AROUND THE NATIONAL GALLERIES OF SCOTLAND

BY EILIDH MULDOON

THE NATIONAL GALLERIES OF SCOTLAND ARE FULL OF WONDERFUL THINGS TO SEE. SOMEWHERE THERE IS A STATUE OF FAMOUS SCOTTISH POET ROBERT BURNS...

...CAN YOU FIND IT?

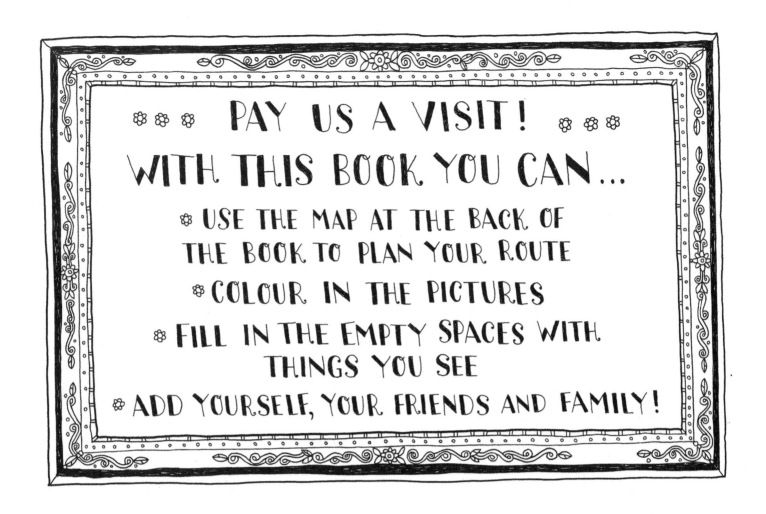

PAY US A VISIT!

WITH THIS BOOK YOU CAN...

- USE THE MAP AT THE BACK OF THE BOOK TO PLAN YOUR ROUTE
- COLOUR IN THE PICTURES
- FILL IN THE EMPTY SPACES WITH THINGS YOU SEE
- ADD YOURSELF, YOUR FRIENDS AND FAMILY!

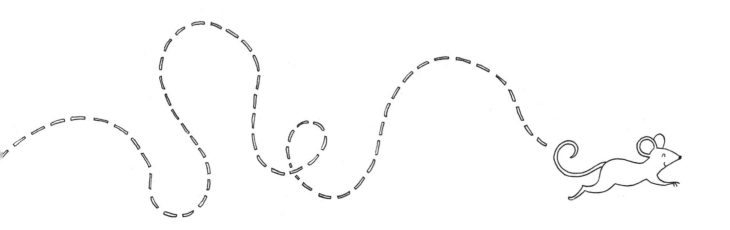

MODERN
TWO

PAOLOZZ

THIS WAY U

PORTRAIT
GALLERY

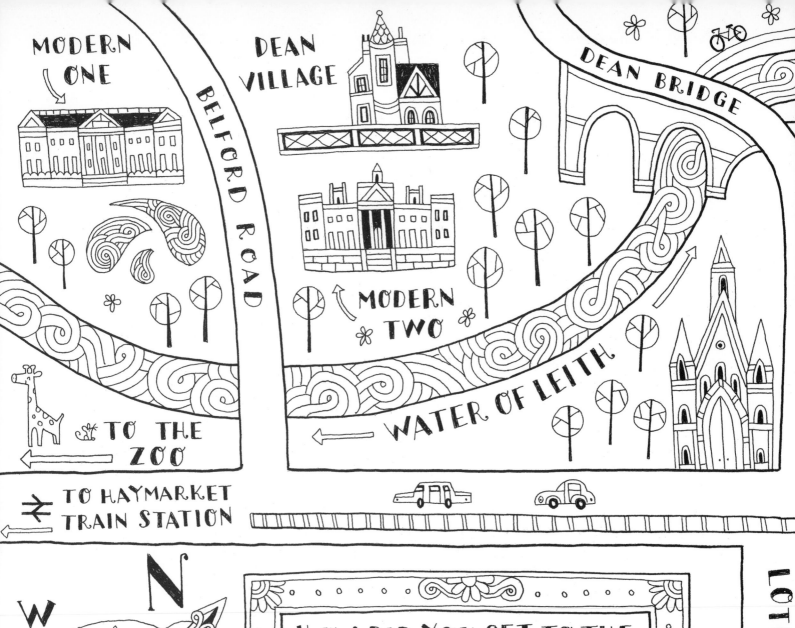

MODERN ONE

BELFORD ROAD

DEAN VILLAGE

DEAN BRIDGE

MODERN TWO

WATER OF LEITH

TO THE ZOO

TO HAYMARKET TRAIN STATION

W N E S

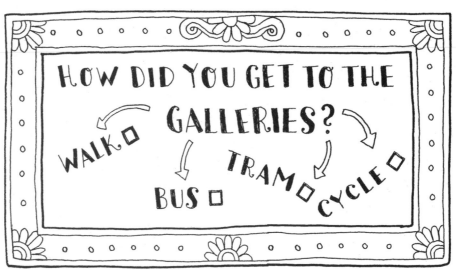

HOW DID YOU GET TO THE GALLERIES?

WALK ☐

BUS ☐

TRAM ☐

CYCLE ☐

LOTHIAN ROAD

GALLERY GUIDE

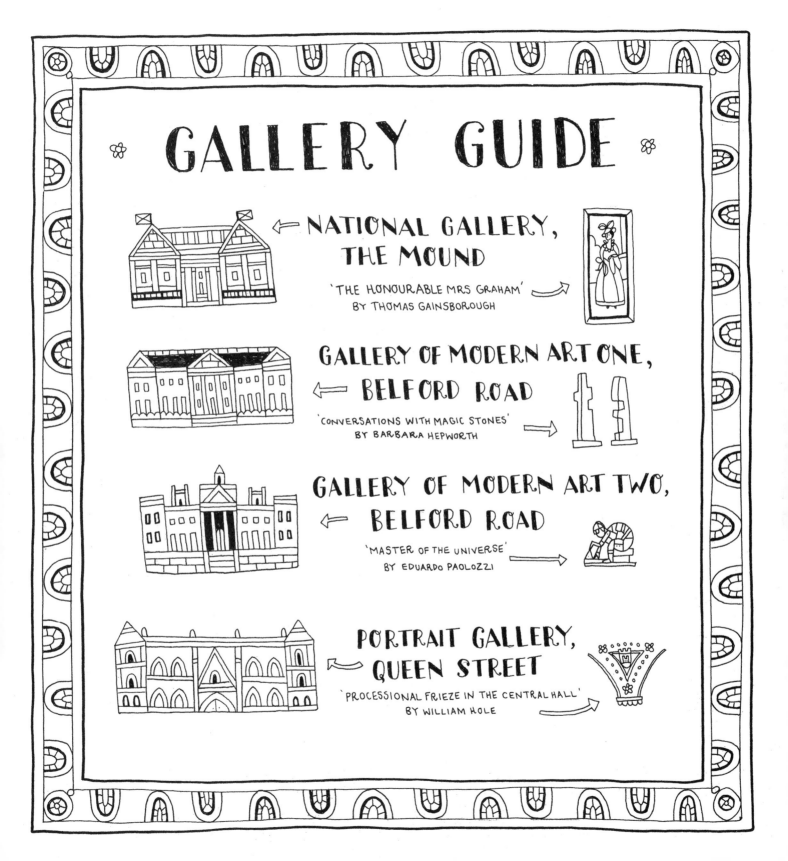

NATIONAL GALLERY, THE MOUND
'THE HONOURABLE MRS GRAHAM' BY THOMAS GAINSBOROUGH

GALLERY OF MODERN ART ONE, BELFORD ROAD
'CONVERSATIONS WITH MAGIC STONES' BY BARBARA HEPWORTH

GALLERY OF MODERN ART TWO, BELFORD ROAD
'MASTER OF THE UNIVERSE' BY EDUARDO PAOLOZZI

PORTRAIT GALLERY, QUEEN STREET
'PROCESSIONAL FRIEZE IN THE CENTRAL HALL' BY WILLIAM HOLE

TO THE BOTANIC GARDENS

TO LEITH

PORTRAIT GALLERY

ST ANDREW SQUARE

LEITH STREET

PLAYHOUSE

BUS STATION

TO CALTON HILL

TO HOLYROOD PALACE

& ARTHUR'S SEAT

WAVERLEY TRAIN STATION

MY ART ADVENTURE

FILL THIS SPACE WITH DOODLES ↗

FOR A COMPLETE LIST OF CURRENT PUBLICATIONS PLEASE WRITE TO: NGS PUBLISHING, SCOTTISH NATIONAL GALLERY OF MODERN ART, 75 BELFORD ROAD, EDINBURGH EH4 3DR. OR VISIT OUR WEBSITE: WWW.NATIONALGALLERIES.ORG

NATIONAL GALLERIES OF SCOTLAND IS A CHARITY REGISTERED IN SCOTLAND (NO. SC003728)